GOD IS CALLING YOU, WILL YOU ANSWER THE CALL?

USING YOUR GIFTS, ABILITIES AND TALENTS FOR THE KINGDOM OF GOD

CARLA STROGEN

Unless otherwise indicated, all scripture quotations are taken from the King James Version of the Bible.

God Is Calling You
Will You Answer The Call?
ISBN: 978-7344020-0-1
Copyright 2020 Carla Strogen

Graphic design done by Fiverr

Printed in the United States of America.

All rights reserved. This material is protected by the United States copyright laws. No part of this publication may be reproduced, stored in a retrieval system or transmitted in any form or by any means, electronic, mechanical or photocopying, recording, or otherwise without the prior permission of the publisher.

CONTENTS

Acknowledgements 5

Foreword 7

Endorsements 9

Introduction 11

The Call 15

Will You Answer The Call? 23

Chapter 1: Prayer 31

Chapter 2: Reading, Studying and
Confessing the Word of God 39

Chapter 3: Fasting 49

Conclusion 53

Prayer 59

Prayer of Salvation 61

Notes 63

ACKNOWLEDGEMENTS

I thank Christ Jesus, my Lord, who hath enabled me, for that he counted me faithful, putting me into the ministry. (1 Timothy 1:12)

I want to thank my mother, Georgia M. Mack, my family and friends for your love and support. In loving memory of my twin sister, Paula Flournoy.

I want to thank my Pastors, Apostle Al & Pastor Alice Hall and Apostle Carl & Pastor Hattie Franklin for your words of wisdom and encouragement.

I want to thank my husband, Prophet Sedirk Strogen for being a loving, supportive and encouraging husband.

I want to thank all those who have spoken into my life over the years. I pray God's blessings over all your lives.

FOREWORD

As you open the pages of God Is Calling You, Will You Answer The Call? You will find yourself immersed in a life change. Prophetess Carla Strogen is being used by God to radically impact a generation of young people who have been broken by life. Just as we all use to be.

Through the years I have know many women leaders and watched them emerge into their ministries. Prophetess Carla Strogen is using her gifts, abilities and talents for the kingdom of God.

She shares her own journey openly, leaving you hungry to know Him more. She will encourage you to press into more of what God has promised. To know Him clearly and reveal His nature is our greatest responsibility. The Holy Spirit took up residence inside you when you became a follower of Jesus.

Prophetess Carla all of heaven has positioned itself to watch what you will accomplish in His name.

Apostle Carl Franklin
Fountain Of Life Kingdom Church

ENDORSEMENTS

The material in this book challenges you to take a deeper look at the CALL God has on your life. Prophetess Carla Strogen brilliantly demonstrates personal insights that will open our eyes. A must read, and I recommend for those who have a hunger to answer the CALL.

Apostle Al Hall
Pastor/Teacher
Believers International Fellowship

It has been such a pleasure for us to know Prophetess Carla Strogen and now to read her book, God Is Calling You, Will You Answer The Call? Both her personal ministry as well as her writing carry such an impartation of the Father's jovial heart toward His children. Seek ye first the kingdom of God, God desires of us that we put Him first in our lives. I have known Prophetess Carla Strogen since 1998. This book will draw you close intimacy by ushering you in the presence of God. I highly recommend this book. Learn how to speak and apply the word of God to create the life you desire.

Pastor Hattie Franklin
Fountain Of Life Kingdom Church

But as it is written, eye hath not seen, nor ear heard, neither have entered into the heart of man, the things which God hath prepared for them that love him. But God hath revealed them unto us by his Spirit: for the Spirit searcheth all things, yea, the deep things of God

(1 Corinthians 2:9,10)

INTRODUCTION

God has called each of us to do something in the ministry. It may be apostle, prophet, evangelist, pastor, Sunday school teacher, usher, choir member, intercessor, nursery worker, or ministry of helps. You must ask God to reveal your purpose. He will shew you, if you seek him.

And he gave some apostles; and some prophets; and some, pastors and teachers; For the perfecting of the saints, for the work of the ministry, for the edifying of the body of Christ (Ephesians 4:11-12).

Now we are the body of Christ, and members in particular. And God hath set some in the church, first apostles, secondarily prophets, thirdly teachers, after that miracles, then gifts of healings, helps, governments, diversities of tongues. (1 Corinthians 12:27-28).

How do you become who God has called you to be? How do you overcome challenges and obstacles when faced with issues of life? You need help beyond your ability to do what God has called you to do, and that help come from Holy Spirit (your leader, guide, helper and comforter).

But the Comforter, which is the Holy Ghost, whom the Father will send in my name, he shall teach you all things, and bring all things to your remembrance, whatsoever I have said unto you (John 14:26).

It is so important to be filled with Holy Spirit. If you are not filled with Holy Spirit, you can be. Ask for the gift.

If ye then, being evil, know how to give good gifts unto your children: how much more shall your heavenly Father give the Holy Spirit to them that ask him? (Luke 11:13)

We need power to do the work of the kingdom, power only comes through Holy Spirit.

But ye shall receive power, after that the Holy Ghost is come upon you: and ye shall be witnesses unto me both in Jerusalem, and in all Judea, and in Samaria, and unto the uttermost part of the earth (Acts 1:8).

You can pray in the Spirit. You might ask, how do you do that?

And they were all filled with the Holy Ghost, and began to speak with other tongues, as the Spirit gave them utterance (Acts 2:4).

First, you must be filled with the Holy Spirit. Jude 1:20, But ye beloved, building up yourselves on your most holy faith, praying in the Holy Ghost.

If you feel that you can't walk in the gifts and calling God has purposed for your life, I am here to encourage you, and say yes you can do it.

You can do all things through Christ which strengthens you (Philippians 4:13).

This is one of my favorite scriptures that helped me when I felt like I could not do this. Holy Spirit would remind me and say yes you can.

Lo, I am with you always, even unto the end of the world (Matthew 28:20). He is with you at all times. It is growing process, and I am ever learning. I am so amazed how far I have matured.

THE CALL

At a young age, I realized I was different, but I did not totally understand the call that God had on my life. At the age of thirteen, I would read the bible, and pray on a regular basis, but I really did not have any understanding of the word of God. I would have a desire to get in the presence of God, and I did not understand what was happening during this time. Now, I look back and understand why I did the things I did. I tried to fit in with the crowd, but I just did not feel comfortable. I would go to parties, but I really did not want to be there. I would go and stand on the wall the entire time I was there. I was asked to dance, and I would say no. I did not have any rhythm anyway, so it really did not matter if I danced or not. The entire time I was there I was saying in my mind; I am ready to go. I did not have a desire to drink or smoke, thank God. I made a decision that I was not having sex until I was married. I am a testimony that it is possible, if you want to be kept God will help you. Everything we do, it's our choice. God will not override your will. It was certain things I had purposed I was just not going to do. I thank God for keeping me.

As a teenager, I began to visit different churches that explained the word of God on a different level, and I became more knowledgeable of biblical principles. I did not have an understanding about the gifts of the Spirit. As I began to attend churches that taught that these gifts do operate in the church today through anointed men and women of God, I began to understand these biblical principles. I didn't have a clue.

1 Corinthians Chapter 12 explains spiritual gifts.

For to one is given by the Spirit the word of wisdom; to another the word of knowledge by the same Spirit; to another faith by the same Spirit; to another the gifts of healing by the same Spirit; to another the working of miracles; to another prophecy; to another discerning of spirits; to another divers kinds of tongues; to another the interpretations of tongues (1 Corinthians 12:8-10).

This was all new to me, but I began to understand the word of God more clearly. I began to grow spiritually. I began to see another side of God that I had never experienced before. I would go to revivals, and I would get prophecies from different men and women of God about how God would use me in the gift of prophecy, and I had a calling on my life. Now, I am trying to process this, and ponder in my mind how is all this going to happen. I graduated high school, and then I went to college. I am still committed to God. I attended a Friday night church service. I was prophesied to again about the calling on my life. I couldn't get away from it. God was still reminding me of the call. When I was told I would prophesy, I was like God not me, I can't do that.

You need someone in your life that see your potential beyond what you see. God will use others to provoke you to step out of your comfort zone for you to do what God has purposed for your life. I did not even know what the word prophesy meant. According to the King James Dictionary, prophecy is the prediction of something to come. Prophecy is also predestinated words spoken from God into one's life. I would see other people operate in the gift of prophecy, and at the time I did not understand what they were doing. I wondered how they could see and hear from God, but I realized for myself as time went on, it is possible. He was preparing me ahead of time for the call, as those words were spoken over my life because he knew my future. I did not. It was not just going to happen. I had to prepare myself.

As I got in the presence of God in my personal devotional time, I became more sensitive to the voice of God. After I prayed, I would sit and listen. God would begin to talk to me. I kept a journal. I wrote down the words he gave me as he spoke to me. I started writing very few words, and over a period of time the words increased more and more. He would speak to me about myself, and I also began to get prophecies for others as God would lead. I remember the first prophecies I gave was when I was in college in 1991. God would give me words of encouragement for my friends, and they would be amazed, and they would say how did you know I was going through that, I said the Holy Spirit gave it to me. As I began to let the gift of prophecy flow, I began to hear the voice of God more clearly. It is amazing to me how I have become sensitive to the voice of God, and I can hear him talk to me in a still small voice. You might say, does this really happen? Yes, it does. God is no respector of person; he uses those who are willing. You must be willing. God wants you to grow spiritually, and not remain babes in the word.

After I graduated from college, I eventually moved to Shreveport, Louisiana in April 1998. At this time, the ministry I joined helped me continue to grow spiritually. I began to go to prayer service. As time went on, I was one of the ones that prayed before service started. God began to use me to give words of encouragement for my Pastors and others in the ministry. God began to reveal some things to me about my life while I was at this ministry through my Pastors. Again, I was reassured God would use me in the gift of prophecy, and I would minister the word of God one day. I was prophesied to about getting married. There were other prophecies I got as well while I was a member of this church. Everything I was told, came to pass.

If you remain dedicated to God, everything else will be added to you.

But seek ye first the kingdom of God, and his righteousness; and all these things shall be added unto you (Matthew 6:33).

God will give you the desires of your heart. It took years for some of my desires to manifest, but if you remain faithful to God, he will bless you. Did I get discouraged? Yes, many times.

Trust in the Lord, and do good; so shalt thou dwell in the land, and verily thou shalt be fed. Delight thyself also in the Lord; and he shall give thee the desires of thine heart. Commit thy way unto the Lord; trust also in him; and he shall bring it to pass (Psalm 37:3-5).

Just a note to encourage singles to wait on God for your mate. You can't go out and choose. Let God bring your mate to you. He will do it, just trust him in the process. Pray and ask God to send your mate that he has destined for you to marry. You can't force something if it is not a fit. It is not going to work. You will be disappointed and hurt because who you thought was going to be your mate, he is not God's will for your life.

I desired to be married, but I vowed to wait on God to send the right person. My prayer was God don't let me marry the wrong person. I had a confession wrote out about my husband-to-be. First on the list, he had to be saved and dedicated to God. My husband and I dated for one year and seven months before we got engaged.

I got married on June 25, 2015. After I got married, I transitioned to another ministry. After being there a while, I was told that I was going to be given my minister's license. I was like no, I am not ready yet. Then one morning God spoke to me and said it is time, you can't put if off any longer. I said ok God, I will answer the call. On May 7, 2017, I received my Minister's license. On June 25, 2017, on my second wedding anniversary, I ministered my first message. On May 19, 2019 I received my ordination license. My husband and I are a ministry team and we work together. I am truly blessed to see how I have matured over the years. To God be the Glory!

Paul wrote I therefore, the prisoner of the Lord, beseech you that ye walk worthy of the vocation wherewith ye are called, with all lowliness and meekness, with longsuffering, forbearing one another in love. (Ephesians 4:1-2).

But by the grace of God I am what I am and his grace which was bestowed upon me was not in vain (1 Corinthians 15:10).

We must remain humble, and not prideful.

And whosoever shall exalt himself shall be abased; and he that shall humble himself shall be exalted (Matthew 23:12).

My will is to do God's will. I say God not my will, but let your will be done in my life. It is God's will that we continue to grow in our spiritual walk with him.

But grow in grace, and in the knowledge of our Lord and Savior Jesus Christ. To him be glory both now and forever, Amen (2 Peter 3:18).

You can't do it in your own strength. First and foremost, you need God, Holy Spirit and the word of God to help equip you for the call. He gives us what we need, we are the ones that must utilize what we have already been given. Just as the apostles did in the book of Acts 14:3, God is our help as well. Long time therefore abode they speaking boldly in the Lord, which gave testimony unto the word of his grace, and granted signs and wonders to be done by their hands. By God's grace, enabling power they spoke the word of God with great courage and humble confidence because they depended on God for assistance and help. We must do the same, allow God to help us as we minister to others. God has given me boldness to speak before people, and I know Holy Spirit helps me. It is my desire to be obedient to the voice of God and say only what he would have me to say to edify and encourage others.

But he that prophesieth speaketh unto men to edification, and exhortation and comfort (1 Corinthians 14:3).

I began to search the scriptures about prophets and prophetess that was named in the bible and read how God used them in the bible. There are several prophets and prophetess listed in the bible. Anna-prophetess (Luke 2:36-37), Miriam-prophetess (Exodus 15:20), Deborah-prophetess (Judges 4:4), Jeremiah– prophet (Jeremiah 1:5) Ezekiel- prophet (Ezekiel 1), just to name a few.

As newborn babes, desire the sincere milk of the word, that ye may grow thereby (1 Peter 2:2).

For when for the time ye ought to be teachers, ye have need that one teach you again which be the first principles of the oracles of God, and are become such as have need of milk, and not of strong meat. For everyone that useth milk is unskillful in the word of righteousness; for he is a babe. But strong meat belongeth to them that are of full age, even those who by reason of use have their senses exercised to discern both good and evil (Hebrews 5:12-14). God wants us to grow spiritually.

WILL YOU ANSWER THE CALL?

Do you know your assignment? Or have you even asked God this question? When, the gifts lay dormant, this does not bring glory to God. He can't use you if you are resisting the call. Will you answer? Say Yes, Lord I will do what you would have me to do, use me Lord as you will. He only responds through willing vessels. You must realize that you can't do it in your own strength. He gives you the ability to get every assignment done. My grace is sufficient for thee; for my strength is made perfect in weakness. (I Corinthians 12:9)

Don't underestimate yourself. God equips those who He calls for ministry. Ministry is a sacrifice. It will cost you time, and no honestly you will not always feel like it all the time, but you must do it regardless of how you feel. God is not moved by our feelings, but God is moved by our faith. God will give you strength to maintain what he has called you to do.

But without faith it is impossible to please him: for he that cometh to God must believe that he is, and that he is a rewarder of them that diligently seek him (Hebrews 11:6).

This reminds me of the story of Jeremiah, the prophet. He told God he could not speak. He was a child, and that was not the answer God wanted to hear. Jeremiah tried to make excuses, but that did not work. God told Jeremiah that he ordained him to be a prophet to the nations. God knew who Jeremiah was before he spoke those words to him. God reassured Jeremiah that he would use him because he had already equipped him for the call. Is this the way you approach God? You might be looking at your shortcomings, but God knows that you are not perfect. Don't say you can't do it. You may say let someone else do it because they can do it better than you can. You may feel that you are not an eloquent speaker, or you are not ready yet. You may say oh no, I am having so much fun right now.

Not really, as you get older you will see what is important. All that eventually fades away. You do not want to live a live full of regrets. Ask yourself, do you want to live a life full of regrets? Hopefully, your answer is no. I encourage you to live a holy life. Most teenagers and young adults feel that they can't have fun when they become saved. This is not true. You can still have fun and live for Christ. Don't let peer pressure allow you to make the wrong choices in life that you will regret later in your life. If you choose to live a life filled with drinking, drugs, partying, and promiscuity, these activities can lead to problems that you don't want to have to deal with. There are consequences to your actions whether good or bad. Especially, if you hook up with the wrong people. You can be in the wrong place at the wrong time, and the consequences can change your life forever. There are older people that still enjoy the ways of the world. They are not committed totally to God either. You must make up your own mind to be committed to God regardless of what others are doing or not doing. You must give an account to God for yourself, no one else can speak for you. If there was a greater reverence for God some things you would not even consider doing or saying.

The fear of the Lord is to hate evil: pride, and arrogancy, and the evil way, and the forward mouth, do I hate (Proverbs 8:13).

Jesus said unto him, thou shalt love the Lord thy God with all thy heart, and with all they soul, and with all thy mind (Matthew 22:37).

Stop leaning on the crutch God is not finished with me yet, or God knows my heart or I just could not help myself. I just had to lay my religion down. It not about religion. It's about relationship. Stop making excuses to why you still do what you do. Yes, you can help yourself with God, but no you can't trying to do it in your own self. You will fail every time.

All unrighteous is sin (1 John 5:15a).

John 14:15, if you love me, you will keep my commandments.

For if we sin willfully after that we have received the knowledge of the truth, there remaineth no more sacrifice for sins (Hebrews 10:26).

Wherefore come out from among them, and be ye separate, saith the Lord, and touch not the unclean thing; and I will receive you (2 Corinthians 6:17).

You must be totally committed to God. Your actions speak louder than your words. Are you saying one thing out of your mouth and doing something different? Your actions must match what you are saying. God wants us to live godly in this present world. You say is that possible? Yes, it is, but only with God's help. You can do it.

For the grace of God that bringeth salvation hath appeared to all men, teaching us that, denying ungodliness and worldly lusts, we should live soberly, righteously, and godly, in this present world. (Titus 2:11-12).

One bad decision can change your life for the rest of your life.

Experience is a teacher, but experience is not the best teacher. You learn the lesson afterwards, when you can prevent that if you listen first. You will not have to go through certain things if you take heed to others advice on what to do, and what not to do. Don't learn the hard way. Be wise and take preventative actions.

I beseech you therefore, brethren, by the mercies of God, that ye present your bodies a living sacrifice, holy, acceptable unto God, which is your reasonable service. And be ye transformed by the renewing of your mind, that ye may prove what is that good, and acceptable, and perfect, will of God. (Romans 12:1-2)

Poverty and shame shall be to him that refuseth instruction: but he that regardeth reproof shall be honoured. (Proverbs 13:18)

Of course, we all make mistakes. We are not perfect. It is not hard to live a Christian life. It is all about having a will to do it. Holy Spirit is our keeper. There are people who feel they can't dedicate themselves to God because they are not ready to be committed to God. How much time do you need? Don't wait until you get in a crisis, and then give your life to Christ. He rather you get saved before you experience some adverse situation. I will say again you do not want to have any regrets in life. God uses willing vessels, and he will not force you to do anything against your will. Be willing, and let God handle the rest. He gives you the ability to make your own choices. He is just that kind of God. Remember, there are consequences that follow each decision you make, rather it is good or bad.

You should have the same tenacity and passion for God as you do for the things of the world. No questions ask, when you enjoy doing those things you like to do. You give your all for your hobbies, passions, playing your favorite sport, video games or whatever it may be. Time and place are no issue. You will travel near and far to get to an event. No matter if it's raining, sleeting or snowing. If you can make it, you are going regardless. What about God? What is your attitude when it comes to what God's will is for your life? Don't give God less, when you give the world your best. Don't forget about God when you get what you want.

For what is a man profited, if he shall gain the whole world, and lose his own soul? or what shall a man give in exchange for his soul? (Matthew 16:26)

I call heaven and earth to record this day against you, that I have set before you life and death, blessing and cursing: therefore choose life, that both thou and thy seed may live. (Deuteronomy 30:19)

He gives you a choice, but he makes it clear which to choose. He says choose life.

Choose you this day whom you will serve. Let's be like Joshua, he said As for me and my house we will serve the Lord. (Joshua 24:15).

Say, I can do all things through Christ which strengthens me. (Philippians 4:13).

What is your testimony? What kind of life are you living?

Wherefore also we pray always for you, that our God would count you worthy of this calling, and fulfill all the good pleasure of his goodness, and the work of faith with power. That the name of our Lord Jesus Christ may be glorified in you, and ye in him, according to the grace of our God and the Lord Jesus Christ. (1 Thessalonians 1: 11-12)

It should be to live a life pleasing to God like the men and women spoken of in Hebrews chapter 11:1-13, they obtain a good report. Their lives were a reflection of the word of God, and their faith in God.

1. Now faith is the substance of things hoped for, the evidence of things not seen.
2. For by it the elders obtained a good report.
3. Through faith we understand that the worlds were framed by the word of God, so that things which are seen were not made of things which do appear.
4. By faith Abel offered unto God a more excellent sacrifice than Cain, by which he obtained witness that he was righteous, God testifying of his gifts: and by it he dead yet speaketh.
5. By faith Enoch was translated that he should not see death; and was not found, because God has translated him: for before his translation he had this testimony, that he pleased God.
6. But without faith it is impossible to please him: for he that cometh to God must believe that he is, and that he is a rewarder of them that diligently seek him.
7. By faith Noah, being warned of God of things not seen as yet, moved with fear, prepared an ark to the saving of his house; by the which he condemned the world, and became heir of the righteous which is by faith.

8. By faith Abraham, when he was called to go out into a place which he should after receive for an inheritance, obeyed; and he went out, not knowing whither he went.
9. By faith he sojourned in the land of promise, as in a strange country, dwelling in tabernacles with Isaac and Jacob, the heirs with him of the same promise:
10. For he looked for a city which hath foundations, whose builder and maker is God.
11. Through faith also Sara herself received strength to conceive seed and was delivered of a child when she was past age, because she judged him faithful who had promised.
12. Therefore, sprang there even of one, and him as good as dead, so many as the stars of the sky in multitude, and as the sand which is by the seashore innumerable.
13. These all died in faith, not having received the promises, but having seen them afar off, and were persuaded of them, and embraced them, and confessed that they were strangers and pilgrims on the earth.

These men and women lived their lives by faith. Awesome men and women of God that was moved by faith and not by what they saw.

I will share with you three principles that helped me grow spiritually and develop my personal relationship with God. These principles helped me stay focus when I experience adverse situation in my life. The three principles are spending time in prayer, reading, studying and confessing the word of God, and fasting. My prayer is as you utilize these principles you will develop your spiritual commitment to God on a greater level.

Chapter 1

PRAYER

It is important to start your day with prayer. Prayer will equip you for what lies ahead because you never know what will take place from day today. The number one key is to develop a personal relationship with God. You can't rely on someone else's prayers, but you must know God for yourself. He speaks to your spirit man. Your carnal (human ability or reasoning) mind will not understand the spiritual things of God.

But the natural man does not understand the spiritual things of God, for they are foolishness to him; nor can he know them, because they are spiritually discerned. (1 Corinthians 2:14).

You may try to rationalize things in your carnal mind, but you will not comprehend the spiritual realm with your carnal mind. It is impossible to do.

Because the carnal mind is enmity against God; for it is not subject to the law of God, neither indeed can be (Romans 8:7).

Your flesh will constantly fight against the things of God. You are made up of a three part being which consists of a soul (mind, will and emotions, and intellect), spirit (commune with God), and body (consist of senses).

And the very God of peace sanctify you wholly; and I pray God your whole spirit and soul and body be preserved blameless unto the coming of our Lord Jesus Christ (1 Thessalonians 5:23).

Jesus said unto him, thou shalt love the Lord thy God with all they heart, and with all thy soul, and with all thy mind. This is the first and greatest commandment (Matthew 22: 37, 38).

You go to church on Sunday morning and mid-week service on Wednesday and say that is all the time I need to give God. Or maybe you go to church every now and then. You say oh, God understands. I am just a busy person. No, that is not enough time to give God. You must do more than the norm. You must also designate other times to get in the presence of God. If you know you will have a busy morning ahead of you, get up earlier to pray. You might have to stay up later at night in order to spend time in prayer. Do what works for you.

You can do it, sacrifice your time for God. You can find the time to do everything else that you want to do. You must keep your spirit man built up so when test and trials come you will know how to deal with problems and situations. You must know what the word says in order to pray the word of God. Remember, you are victorious no matter what you go through. When it looks like nothing is happening, you must know that God will make a way for you. He takes what looks impossible and makes possible.

Behold, I will do a new thing; now it shall spring forth; shall ye not know it I will even make a way in the wilderness, and rivers in the desert. (Isaiah 43:19)

God will hear your prayer if you ask in faith, and it is according to His will.

And this is the confidence that we have in him, that if w ask any thing according to his will, he heareth us: And if we know that he hear us, whatsoever we ask, we know that we have the petitions that we desired of him 1 John 5:14,15).

You must know that you will be delivered out of whatever situation you are in.

For verily I say unto you, That whosoever shall say unto this mountain, Be thou removed, and be thou cast into the sea; and shall not doubt in his heart, but shall believe that those things which he saith shall come to pass, he shall have whatsoever he saith. Therefore, I say unto you, what things soever ye desire, when ye pray, believe that ye receive them, and ye shall have them. (Mark 11:23, 24)

The more you began to spend time in prayer, you will begin to hear the voice of God more clearly. It takes discipline to sit and listen quietly in the presence of God. He also enables you to minister to others in the time of their need. For example, with a relationship between a man and woman, you must spend quality time with that person in order for the relationship to grow. Over a period of time, you began to express to one another how you feel about each other, and you enjoy being in that person presence. God wants the same type of commitment by spending quality time with him, and for you to have a desire to know more about him. He wants you to recognize him as God the Father, Son and Holy Spirit. You must let him know that He is a great and awesome God. Holy Spirit will begin to share spiritual revelation with you, as you began to develop a closer relationship with God. Your spiritual eyes and ears will be open clearly. I know this probably sounds strange to some of you, but it happens. Pray

Ephesians 1:17-21, Colossians 1:9-14 and Isaiah 11:2. These prayers are for wisdom and revelation knowledge to know God in a greater way. In order to become sensitive to the voice of God, it requires much discipline. No, it is not always easy to pray. Sometimes you will have to pray, and you may feel like that it is the most inopportune time. Especially, if you are watching your favorite TV show or doing chores around the house, tending to your children, or whatever it may be. You can become occupied with a lot of other things and spend many hours in a day staying busy doing something. It is a never-ending cycle. You say ok God, I will pray when I finish this, or when I finish that. By then you are too tired to do anything else. You offer God a few minutes of your time, and you are not really focused on praying because you probably will fall asleep from being too exhausted. God wants quality time which is time set aside just for Him. It is important that you move when God says so. Especially, if you really get an unction, or urge to pray. I will say again this only happens through discipline.

As an intercessor, I learned the importance of prayer. You may say what is an intercessor. An intercessor is one who pleads on behalf of another, to make a petition for others.

Jesus prays to the Father on our behalf. He is our advocate. He is there present before God to present our petitions, to plead on our behalf.

Who is he that condemneth? It is Christ that died, yea rather, that is risen again, who is even at the right hand of God, who also maketh intercession for us (Romans 8:34).

Scriptures on intercession:

I exhort therefore, that first of all, supplications, prayers, intercession giving of thanks, be made for all men (1 Timothy 2:1).

Again, I say unto you. That if two of you shall agree on earth as touching anything that they shall ask, it shall be done for them of my Father which is in heaven. For where two or three are gathered together in my name, there am I in the midst of them (Matthew 18:19,20).

But I have prayed for thee, that thy faith fail not; and when thou are coverted, strengthen they brethren (Luke 22:32.)

Praying always with all prayer and supplication in the Spirit and watching thereunto with all perseverance and supplication for all saints (Ephesians 6:18).

Once during my prayer time, I had an encounter as I was in the presence of God. The power of God was so strong that I literally felt I were miles away in the spirit realm, and all I could see were bright lights, pure white surrounding me. After this experience, the power of God was still strong upon me that both of my hands were burning with heat. It was like I had been in a whirlwind; I was dizzy. The power of God's presence was so strong, and it will be an experience that I will never forget. God wants to reveal Himself to you on a personal level. The power of God is real.

You may wonder how some people flow in their calling, and it looks like they are dealing with no struggles. It looks like they never go through anything. You will be surprised. They are faced with many oppositions, but as you reach a level of maturity in your spiritual walk over time, you will know how to deal with the situations and not make it so obvious that you are going through a trial. When I first started praying before the congregation, I would be so nervous that my hands began to sweat. My heart began to beat fast, and my voice started trembling. There were times that Satan would attack my mind just before I would get up to pray and fear would grip me. I began to pray, and ask God to help me before I started to pray, I quoted, for God hath not given me the spirit of fear; but of power, and of love, and of a sound mind. 2 Timothy 1:7. When I finished, I was like whew I made it. I was not use to being in front a lot of people, that was a challenge. I am a shy person when it comes to standing in front of people anyway. I never was one who liked to speak before people, but with God help I can. Now, I look back and I see how much I have matured. It amazes me, to God be the glory. I realize God will equip you for the call. He has given you spiritual weapons to fight the battle against the enemy.

Finally, my brethren, be strong in the Lord, and in the power of his might. Put on the whole armour of God which is our loins girt about with truth and having on the breastplate of righteous, our feet shod with the preparation of the gospel of peace, and the shield of faith, the helmet of salvation and the sword of the spirit, which is the word of God. Praying always with all prayer and supplication in the Spirit, which is the word of God (Ephesians 6:10-17).

For though we walk in the flesh, we do not war after the flesh: for the weapons of our warfare are not carnal, but mighty through God to the pulling down of strongholds; casting down imaginations, and every high thing that exalteth itself against the knowledge of God, and bringing into captivity every thought to the obedience of Christ (1 Corinthians 10:4,5.)

Praise and worship should also be a part of your prayer time. The book of Psalm have many of scriptures on praise and worship.

But the hour cometh, and now is, when the true worshippers shall worship the Father in spirit and in truth: for the Father seeketh such to worship him. God is a Spirit: and they that worship him must worship him in spirit and in truth. (John 4:23,24)

O come, let us worship and bow down: let us kneel before the Lord our maker. (Psalm 95:6)

Praise ye the Lord. O give thanks unto the Lord; for he is good: for his mercy endureth forever. (Psalm 106:1)

You should not have a problem praising God, and to give him the glory for his goodness he has shown towards you. Praise is to thank God for what he has done, what he is doing, and that he is going to do in your life. You must praise him before the manifestation, and not wait until the blessing manifest, that's faith. Holy Spirit revealed to me one day that praise gets God's attention, and faith move the hand of God to release the blessing in our life. God is so good, and that is why you should let him know how much you love and appreciate him for all he does. What happen in Joshua chapter 6 when the wall of Jericho fell. Joshua had to have faith in what God told them to do in order to receive the blessing. Joshua and the Israelite army marched around the city and blew their trumpets and praised God and the wall fell just like God told them it would. Praise leads us into worship. Worship expresses to God who he is.

Which in his times he shall shew, who is the blessed and only Potentate, the Kings of kings, and Lord of lords. (1 Timothy 6:15)

This is a form of worship because this scripture states who God is. You might say is praise and worship necessary, yes, it is. As you began to spend time with God by getting into his presence and worship him, he began to talk to you. Yes, this really does happen. God desires to reveal himself to you on a greater level, but you must be a willing vessel. You must make the sacrifice to do what it takes to get these results to manifest in your life. It just does not automatically happen.

Chapter 2

READING, STUDYING AND CONFESSING THE WORD OF GOD

The word of God is a very vital part of our lives. It helps us to make it through the challenges that we face daily. As you read the word of God, it causes you to focus on how you should live as a Christian, and why you should live accordingly. The word of God must be applied in order to see results. Reading the word is not enough. You must be a doer of the word. God is faithful to his word, but we you must do your part as a believer. In order to grow you must study the word of God for yourself, and not depend on others.

Study to shew thyself approved unto God, a workman that needeth not to be ashamed, rightly dividing the word of truth (2 Timothy 2:15).

But be ye doers of the word, and not hearers only, deceiving you own selves (James 1:22).

Your lifestyle should be different from the world. You can't say and do some things that you use to because you should be an example to them. You are saved now, born again. There should be some evidence of a holy lifestyle. You are in the world, but not of the world.

God wants us to be changed in his image.

But we all, with open face beholding as in a glass the glory of the Lord, are changed into the same image from glory to glory, even as by the Spirit of the Lord. (2 Corinthians 3:18)

And be not conformed to this world: but be ye transformed by the renewing of your mind, that ye may prove what that is good, and acceptable, and perfect, will of God. (Romans 12:2).

Our mind must be renewed with God's way of doing things because some things that were taught was contrary to the word of God. If your mind is not renewed there will be no change.

Beware lest any man spoil you through philosophy and vain deceit, after the tradition of men, after the rudiment of the world, and not after Christ. (Colossians 2:8)

What about your love walk? This is a challenge if you don't have God's help. Especially if someone has done you wrong, and you have been nothing but good to them. How do you respond? No, it is not easy, but it is possible to do with the help of the Holy Spirit. You must be willing to forgive.

Dearly beloved avenge not yourselves, but rather give place into wrath: for it is written, vengeance is mine; I will repay, saith the Lord (Romans 12:19).

When a man's ways please the Lord, he maketh even his enemies to be at peace with him (Proverbs 16:7).

Sometimes you do find yourself saying things that you should not, but God will help you deal with the issues.

Charity suffered long and is kind; charity envieth not; charity vaunteth not itself, is not puffed up, doth not behave itself unseemly, seek not her own, is not easily provoked, thinketh no evil. (1 Corinthians 13:4, 5)

Sometimes people will not like you for any reason at all, and you may not have done that person any wrong. People become jealous for many reasons. It could be that you are walking in the blessings of God, or a position that they thought they deserved, but you got it instead.

For we wrestle not against flesh and blood, but against principalities, against powers, against rulers of darkness of this world, against spiritual wickedness in high places. (Ephesians 6:12).

Whatever you are tempted with there is an answer in the bible. You must know what the word says in order to act on the word. You must study the word for yourself. Whatever you are dealing with, find a scripture and confess the word of God about your situation.

It is good to purchase other inspirational reading material also because these books help encourage you in your daily walk with God. You can read the bible, and you may not be as focused, but try to read daily devotional books, and other prayer books that will help you understand what you are reading. As you confess and meditate and get the word in your spirit man, Holy Spirit can bring to your remembrance the word of God as it relates to those situations and circumstances that you are going through. What you confess become your reality. Words are powerful. In spite of the problems and situations, you encounter you must choose to say what the word says. Speak to the problem, speak life. Confess what you want to manifest, and not what you don't want to manifest. No matter what it looks like in the natural, or no matter what you feel like, keep confessing the word.

This Book of the Law shall not depart from your mouth, but you shall meditate in it day and night, that you may observe to do according to all that is written in it. For then you make your make prosperous, and then you will have good success. (Joshua 1:8)

You can't take reading and studying the word of God lightly because you must remember we have an adversary. The enemy may attack you in the area of depression, anxiety, sickness or disappointments and the list goes on and on. There is nothing that you can't stand against with God on your side. Sometimes, it looks like you will not make it through the test and trials you face, but God will make a way of escape every time. You must remember what the word of God says about Satan.

The thief comes to steal, and to kill, and to destroy, but God have come that we may have life, and we may have it more abundantly. (John 10:10)

Therefore, you must use the word of God against Satan's tricks and plots. Don't back down against the enemy because you have authority over him. There is nothing you can't handle with God on your side. You know, there are times that we don't read the bible the way we should. Holy Spirit will remind us this is the only way you will be able to come through every trial and test. Christianity is not a religion, but a lifestyle. You must have a personal relationship with the Father yourself. You must live according to the word of God, not just talk it.

You should take on the character and attributes of Christ. You will not be able to resist the enemy if you do not have the word of God within you to resist the enemy. You will be move by what your flesh wants to do, or you will be move by what you hear and see in the natural. The word of God is one of the weapons that you can use when you are going through trials and tribulations. Jesus used the word on the devil when he was led into the wilderness by the Holy Spirit to be tempted by the devil. (Matthew Chapter 4). You must confess the word of God over your situations and circumstances. When you don't see any results right away, you must continue to stand on the word. How do you think Jesus survived the test? He reminded the devil what the word of God says. He told him "It is written" The word gives you hope and strength to endure until your breakthroughs manifest. Because we live in a fleshly body, we will fall short, but God is merciful to forgive. He will allow us to repent.

If we confess our sins, He is faithful and just to forgive us for our sins and cleanse us from all unrighteous. (1 John 1:9)

Don't take grace for granted, just because God forgives. When you know better you do better.

Therefore, to him that knoweth to do good, and doeth it not, to him it is sin. (James 4:17)

When I was a child, I spake as a child, I understood as a child, I thought as a child: but when I became a man, I put away childish things. (1 Corinthians 13:11)

There are many examples of great men and women of God today that you can pattern your life after that have been tried and tested and survived the storms of life. They have proven that God's word is forever settled, if God said it, he will make it good. I can testify of how God have brought me out of so many trials and test. I know if it was not for Him, I would not have made it. There were times I cried, but I had to realize my tears would not move God. I had to rely on the word of God, and my faith to bring me out. There were times I did not have enough money to pay my bills. I had to confess scriptures on finances in order to get my breakthrough.

But my God shall supply all your need according to his riches in glory by Christ Jesus. (Philippians 4:19)

There were times I needed a healing in my body, and I had to know what the word of God says about healing in order to receive my healing.

But he was wounded for our transgressions, he was bruised for our iniquities, the chastisement of our peace was upon him; and with his stripes we are healed. (Isaiah 53:5)

God made a way every time I needed Him. He always will, if you remain faithful to him.

Many are the afflictions of the righteous: but the Lord delivereth him out of them all. (Psalm 34:19)

There were times I was trying to fix my own problems and not relying on God. The devil would tell me, I didn't have to pay my tithes because I needed the money to pay my bills. I will say, I was contemplating hard not to pay my tithes, but the devil was defeated.

I paid my tithes. God would always make a way for my needs to be met. People would come up to me, and they would say God told me to bless you, and they would put money in my hands, or I received an unexpected check in the mail. It would be right when I needed it. I can remember there was a time I did not even know what paying tithes was, but thank God for revelation, now I know. Tithe is ten percent of your income. It may seem like there is no hope, but trust God and watch Him move on your behalf.

What does God say about paying tithes? Why is paying tithes is necessary? These next scriptures will answer these questions.

Will a man rob God? Yet ye have robbed me. But ye say, wherein have we robbed thee? In tithes and offerings. Ye are cursed with a curse: for ye have robbed me, even this whole nation. Bring ye all the tithes into the storehouse, that there may be meat in mine house and prove me now herewith, saith the Lord of hosts, if I will not open you the windows of heaven, and pour you out a blessing that there shall be not room enough to receive it. And I will rebuke the devourer for your sakes, and he shall not destroy the fruits of your ground; neither shall your vine cast her fruit before the time in the field, saith the Lord of hosts. And all nations shall call you blessed: for ye shall be a delightsome land, saith the Lord of hosts. (Malachi 3:8-12).

When you meet the conditions for giving, you must call forth your harvest from your seed that you have sown financially.

Give and it shall be given unto you; good measure, pressed down, and shaken together, and running over, shall men give into your bosom. For with the same measure that ye mete withal it shall be measured to you again. (Luke 6:38)

I made a decision to make a demand on the seed that I had sown and confess the word of God. I remember my twin sister and I had just graduated college, and we needed a vehicle. We were trying to get established and find a job. We were given 1984 Cutlass, gray, 2 doors.

Some probably would say, I don't want to drive nothing like that, but we were grateful to be blessed with a vehicle. We did not have to walk anymore. We drove this car four years. Guess what, the car had no air conditioner, and the gas gauge did not work.

Out of the four years, we ran out of gas only one time. Before then we had to rely on our other sisters for a ride, walk or ride the bus. I remember the times I had to walk to and from work at times, but I made it with God's help. When you go to the car dealership and they say you are denied, sorry we can't help you at this time. What are you going to do? Give up or keep going. I chose to keep going. I remember having to go to a used car lot just to purchase a vehicle. It was not what I wanted at the time, but that was all I could afford. The vehicle had high mileage and had to spend money on it to get certain things fixed. I did not stay in that place because I worked on my credit to get something better. God blessed me to get my first new car in 1999. Even though, I made some bad decisions in my finances, God gave me favor with the car dealership.

So shalt thou find favour and good understanding in the sight of God and man. (Proverbs 3:4)

He is just that awesome. God had already prepared the way for me to purchase the car. I just had to go to the right car dealership. I got discouraged many times, but I knew God had revealed Himself to me over and over again. Satan will try to tell you what you are believing God for will not manifest, but keep confessing the word of God in spite of what it looks like at that moment. No, it will not be easy all the time because we tend to look at the situation in the natural. It looks like there is no hope, but you must look past what is going on in the natural and believe God for a better outcome. He did it for me, and He will do it for you.

He will bless the righteous; with favor thou compass him as with a shield. (Psalm 5:12)

Some things you get are because of the favor of God upon your life. Favor includes good will, kindness, or disposition to oblige another. The word of God will give you instructions on how to make wise decisions in your life.

When it seems like your life is in a state of confusion, and your circumstances and situations are overwhelming, you must trust God's word.

Trust in him with all your heart and lean not to thine own understanding in all thy ways acknowledge him and he will direct your path (Proverbs 3:5, 6).

When you read the word, it will cause you to see how you should respond to situations. I know there were times I would be so frustrated because I was focusing on the problems instead of believing God to change the situation. While waiting for the manifestation of the promise, agree with the word of God. In spite of the oppositions, choose to believe God. Expect God to do exceedingly, abundantly above all you ask or think. The enemy wants us to respond in the natural. He knows if he can break our focus, he got you right where he wants you. No matter what you are dealing with, or you may even be standing in agreement with someone else, continue to stand in faith. It may be finances, healing, salvation or deliverance from drugs or alcohol. Find out what the word says about the situation and continue to confess the word of God. You must stay in agreement with the word of God. You must speak to the problem by confessing the word of God. Ask God for wisdom.

If any of you lack wisdom, let him ask of God, that giveth to all men liberally, and upbraideth not, and it shall be given him (James 1:5).

The bible is our instructions on how to live as a Christian.

All scriptures is given by inspiration of God, and is profitable for doctrine for reproof, for correction, for instructions in righteousness. (2 Timothy 3:16)

As you read the word of God, it allows you to change your mindset and believe what the word of God says about a situation. Then, you will begin to see breakthroughs unfold in your life. So, make it a priority to read, study and confess the word of God daily.

Chapter 3

FASTING

There are many voices that you hear daily. It could be friends, family member, even those you do not know or co-workers. You may receive advice from others, but you want to make sure it is the right advice. Fasting is the third key to become more sensitive to hear the voice of God. What does the bible say about fasting?

That thou appear not unto men to fast, but unto thy Father which is in secret; and thy Father which seeth in secret, shall reward thee openly. (Matthew 6:18)

Is not this the fast that I have chosen? To loose the bands of wickedness, to undo the heavy burdens, and to let the oppressed go free, and that ye break every yoke? (Isaiah 58:6)

And he said unto them, this kind come forth by nothing, but by prayer and fasting. (Mark 9:29)

It allows our spirit man to become more alert and aware to what Holy Spirit wants you to say and do. You will become more sensitive to hear the voice of God. God may tell you to pray for someone or go and visit someone. He is telling you this for a reason, and later you will find out why he told you to do what you did. God will give you instructions for your ministry, and your personal life. He will give you instructions on a certain direction to travel. There were times he told me to go a certain way, but I did not obey. There was an accident ahead, if I would have obeyed, I could have prevented getting stuck in traffic. He will give you plans and ideas on how to do certain things, but you must be in a place to hear him clearly. Fasting is a challenge because you must bring your flesh under subjection. No, I'm not going to say it is easy. Especially, if you are used to eating what you want all the time. If you are like me, I eat three meals a day and snacks in between. Then to say I can't eat anything for a period of time, this is a challenge when you first start fasting. No, it will not be easy to do when you first start, but you will make it. I was like; I don't know if I can handle this one. You will have to sacrifice not eating your favorite meal at times when you really want it. When I started fasting, I would be watching the clock and counting down the time I had left to fast. When I learned how to fast, it was something that I had to learn to do over a period of time, it takes discipline. I started out by not eating for a few hours. As times passed on, I could go half a day and then longer. You will be amazed, as you began to discipline yourself, God will give you the strength to make it through each fast. I remember the times when I would go to eat, and God would say I want you to fast, that sound strange, I know. It has happened to me many times. I would be like God you surely did not say not to eat, this can't be happening as bad as I wanted to eat. I was talking to God like that. Can you imagine while in the process of grabbing your plate and utensils to eat? You hear those words. That was not an easy thing to do. Everything in me wanted to go ahead and eat. My mind was telling me that you can fast another time. This is really when you know you have matured to another level in your spiritual walk. When you walk away and say ok God, I will. When God tell you something like that you would rather ignore that kind of instruction. How will you respond? I will admit there were times I did eat, and I know God was saying fast. I had to repent. God had a purpose for me to fast. There were times when I needed wisdom to make decisions. God told me what to do. He would allow someone with the answer I needed to approach me. I do not believe I would have gotten the answers if I had not spent the quality time fasting and praying to become sensitive to the voice of God. I needed a great move of God because some situations I found myself in, I knew he was the only one that could deliver me out of them. It will take the hand of God to move in some situations that your family and friends can't even help you out of. I was trying to solve my own problems, and I just dug a deeper hole for myself, and it was not easy to get out of. But God. God will help you out of the problems you have created. If you are fasting for manifestations to take place in your life you must have an expectation that it will happen. Faith is what moves God.

For without faith it is impossible to please him, for he who comes to God must believe that he is, and that he is a rewarder of those who diligently seek him. (Hebrews 11:6)

God still blesses you inspite of your shortcomings. He allows you the opportunity to repent and make things right.

CONCLUSION

When you feel like giving up, and you can't go any further, God is there to encourage you. The word of God gives you the strength to make it. When no one else is there to encourage you, you must encourage yourself. You may sometimes ask God why things in your life are not happening the way you think they should? Why are you not seeing the breakthroughs that you desire? You know God has called you to do something, but you do not understand what the calling is. Continue to seek God he will reveal it to you. You have a purpose to fulfill while you are on this earth.

You may say, I am walking in the gifts and calling that God has ordained for me to walk in. I will encourage you to keep doing what you are doing, even though you might get tired, DON'T QUIT.

He giveth power to the faint; and to them that have no might he increaseth strength. Even the youths shall faint and be weary, and the young men shall utterly fall. But they that wait upon the Lord shall renew their strength; they shall mount up with wings as eagles; they shall run, and not be weary; and they shall walk, and not faint (Isaiah 40:29-31).

You will need an extra boost sometimes because you will get physically and mentally tired. Your physical body will resist the things of God. There are times you don't feel like praying, reading, studying the word or fasting.

Satan will try to hinder you from spending time with God. He will try to send all kinds of distractions to break your focus. It is so important to be in a ministry that teaches the principles of the word of God. Isolation is not a good idea. You must be around positive people, and a positive environment that helps you stay focused when you feel like quitting and giving up, and get discouraged. There are times nobody is around; you must encourage yourself.

Do like David did. He encouraged himself.

Why art thou cast down, O my soul? And why art thou disquieted within me? Hope thou in God: for I shall yet praise him, who is the health of my countenance, and my God (Psalm 43:5).

In spite of what he saw in the natural in the city of Ziklag. He still chose to believe God (1 Samuel 30:1-5). Because of His loving-kindness and tender mercies, he shows compassion toward you even when you don't deserve it. When you have not done everything right, He still loves us. How could you not want to be all He has created you to be? You can share with others what Jesus has done for you. Remember whatever God has called you to do, do it as unto the Lord with excellence.

And whatever ye do in word or deed, do all in the name of the Lord Jesus, giving thanks to God and the Father by him (Colossians 3:17)

You must ask God to help you daily because every day you will be tested and tried with something. It could be with your love walk, patience, self-control, longsuffering, temperance, or whatever the case may be. It takes the Holy Spirit to help you respond the right way. We do not always respond the right way in every situation, that is just human nature. You must remain humble before God, and he will help you conquer every battle.

Remember the three important keys that I shared with you that helped me grow spiritually and helps me maintain my walk with God on a daily basis. You must spend time in prayer, read, study and meditate on the word of God, and fast. Watch the manifestations that will take place in your life.

It is a faith walk, no matter what you are believing God to do in your life; you must always exercise your faith because what you see in the natural can be very disappointing.

God is not a man that he should lie, nor a son of man that he should repent has he said, and will he not do? Or has he spoken, and will he not make it good? (Numbers 23:19)

God does not want you to live a defeated life. That is Satan's desire.

The thief cometh not but for to steal, and to kill, and to destroy: I come that they might have life, and that they might have it more abundantly. (John 10:10)

You must remember that Satan has already been defeated. So, we should remind Satan of these words.

Nay in all these things we are more than conquers through him that loved us. (Romans 8:37)

You are victorious. Satan can only get the upper hand if you allow him.

You have power over the enemy. When he tries to attack your mind, and cause you to think that you can't make it. You can remember the past victories that God has brought you through. God is on your side.

If God be for us, then who can be against us. (Romans 8:31) You will not always understand why you go through certain trials and tests. God knows how much you can handle.

There hath no temptation taken you but such as common to man: but God is faithful, who will not suffer you to be tempted above that ye are able; but will with the temptation also make a way to escape, that ye may be able to bear it. (1 Corinthians 10:13)

Some situations may seem overbearing, but you must trust God, and know he is there with you every step of the way. You may often wonder why God must take you the long route before your desires and request are manifested. You must realize he knows best. Sometimes that is hard for us to accept because we want the results instantly. You must endure to receive the reward. It might not happen in 1 week, 1 month, 1 year. It can take years before some of your prayers are answered. You must remain steadfast in the word and know that no matter how long. God is faithful that promise.

Let us hold fast the profession of our faith without wavering; for he is faithful that promised; (Hebrews 10:23).

Know ye not that they which run in a race run all, but one receiveth the prize? So run, that ye may obtain (1 Corinthians 9:24).

The battle is not yours, but God's (1 Chronicles 20:15).

Have you ever tried to solve your own problems? Of course, we all have. Especially, when you think God is taking too long to manifest the answer. You tried to help God out and the situation still did not change.

You must wait and trust God.

Trust in the Lord with all thine heart and lean not to thine own understanding. In all thy ways acknowledge him and he shall direct thy paths (Proverbs 3:5, 6).

You must continue to confess the word no matter what you go through; although you don't feel like it. It may seem that God has forgotten you and left you all alone. He cares for you, and he has your best interest at heart. If you remain faithful to Him, the breakthrough will eventually come. Great is His faithfulness.

For God is not unrighteous to forget your work and labour of love, which ye have shewed toward his name, in that ye have ministered to the saints, and so minister. (Hebrews 6:10)

He desires that every promise come to pass in your life, but you must do your part. Things do not just automatically happen because you want them to. You must expect your prayers to be answered according to the word of God.

The effectual fervent prayer of a righteous man availeth much (James 5:17).

Every good and every perfect gift is from above, and comes down from the Father of lights, with whom is no variableness, neither shadow of turning (James 1:17).

For I know the thoughts that I think toward you, saith the Lord, thoughts of peace and not of evil, to give you an expected end (Jeremiah 29:11).

So shall my word be that goeth forth out of my mouth; it shall not return unto me void, but it shall accomplish that which I please, and it shall prosper in the thing whereunto I sent it (Isaiah 55:11).

Persistence is the key. You can't give up when things are not going right and pull back from God. This is the time when you need to draw closer to him. Therefore, you must continue to stand on God's word and know that he will manifest those prayers and petitions that you have asked of him.

God wants you to live a victorious life. A life that is filled with joy and peace, and have more than enough to be a blessing to his kingdom and others.

Beloved, I wish above all things that thou mayest prosper and be in health, even as thy soul prospereth. (3 John:2)

Always remember, you are more than a conquer though Christ Jesus, and you are victorious in any situation because the greater one lives on the inside of you.

I pray that each of you walk in your calling with full confidence and boldness that you may be a blessing to the body of Christ. I pray the blessings of God would overtake you, and the favor of God rest upon you.

PRAYER

God, I thank you that I am walking in the calling and gifts you have purposed for my life. With you all things are possible. Help me to become the individual you want me to become. I am anointed to do what God has called me to do. I am more than a conquer. I can overcome every obstacle and stumbling block in my life because you are with me, the Lord is my helper. I bind the spirit of fear because God has not given me the spirit of fear, and I loose the power of love and of a sound mind. In the name of Jesus, Amen.

Scriptures:
Matthew 19:26
Romans 8:37
2 Timothy 1:7
Hebrews 13: 5,6

PRAYER OF SALVATION

Romans 10:9

That if thou shalt confess with thy mouth the Lord Jesus, and shalt believe in thine heart that God hath raised him from the dead, thou shalt be saved.

Numbers 6:24-26

The Lord bless thee, and keep thee:
The Lord make his face shine upon thee,
and be gracious unto thee:
The Lord lift up his countenance upon thee, and give thee peace.

NOTES

www.ingramcontent.com/pod-product-compliance
Lightning Source LLC
Chambersburg PA
CBHW021132080526
44587CB00012B/1257